SANDRA SCOFIELD

Busy person's cookbook

FOR BUSY PEOPLE AND WORKING PARENTS

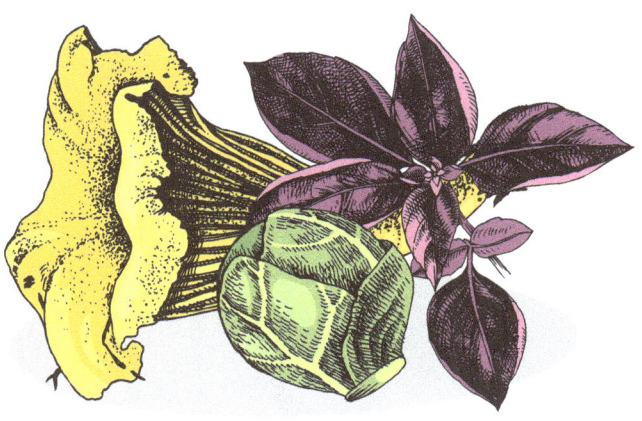

Copyright © Sandra Scofield 2023

All rights reserved. No part of this publication may be reproduced, distributed, or transmitted in any form or by any means, including photocopying, recording, or other electronic or mechanical methods, without the prior written permission of the publisher, except in the case of brief quotations embodied in critical reviews and certain other non-commercial uses permitted by copyright law.

Scofield, Sandra (author)

Busy person's cook book

ISBN 978-1-922890-96-2

Cover and book design by

When you have a busy life,

whether it's because you have kids, work or any of the other things that come at you, sometimes you just run out of time. You want to make nutritious, tasty meals for your family or for yourself, but the clock is against you.

You want to try something new, only to look at a recipe and there is a list of ingredients as long as your arm, thirty minutes of prep time and sixty minutes cook time—really who has the time.

We see meals made on social media or on television in thirty minutes but a lot of the time it is full of pasta or television chefs telling you how easy it is when they probably have an army of people doing their prep.

Inside this book are recipes and meal ideas from busy, everyday people like my mum, my aunty and my work colleagues—just trying to do it all.

All of the recipes will have no more than 6-8 ingredients with very little fuss or mess.

You can add what you like or take out what you don't creating a recipe alternative just for you.

Enjoy!
Sandra

Oven Temperature Guide (electric oven)

I know I still look at recipes from my mum and aunty and the oven temperatures are in Fahrenheit. If you are working with old recipes, here is a Fahrenheit to Celsius conversion to make life simpler.

Temperature Description	Celsius	Fahrenheit
Cool	110	200
Very Slow	120	250
Slow	150	300
Moderate-Slow	180	350
Moderate	200	400
Moderate-Hot	220	425
Hot	230	450
Very Hot	250	475

Measure Equivalents

Cup	Metric	Tbsp	Tsp	Fluid Oz
¼ cup	60 ml	3	12 ½	2
⅓ cup	80 ml	4	16 ½	2 ½
½ cup	125 ml	6	25	4
⅔ cup	160 ml	8	33	5
¾ cup	180 ml	9	37 ½	6
1 cup	250 ml	12 ½	50	8

Just a quick note, the quantity can be varied for how many people you are cooking for.

Entrées

Soups & Salads

ENTRÉES

TIP

When the tomato or BBQ sauce bottle is almost empty add some olive oil, vinegar and any other desired seasoning and shake well. This is an easy salad dressing.

Corn and Celery Salad

INGREDIENTS

440g can corn kernels
1 cup celery
½ cup mayonnaise
1 tbsp parsley
1 tbsp shallots
Salt and pepper to taste

METHOD

1. Chop the celery, parsley and shallots.
2. Mix all of the ingredients together in a bowl.
3. Chill until ready.

ENTRÉES

TIP

You can use black or green olives and add chilli if you would like a bit of kick. I would make a big batch and have them on standby in case we had guests for drinks. Handy to have if putting together an antipasto plate.

Olive Mix

INGREDIENTS

Olive oil
Kalamata olives
1 tbsp brown vinegar
1 clove Garlic, chopped
Pinch of oregano
1 small takeaway food container

METHOD

1. ⅓ fill the takeaway container with olive oil.
2. Add the vinegar, garlic and oregano.
3. Fill the tub with the olives and shake.
4. Let stand for at least 2 hours.

Try adding some black peppercorns as well.

ENTRÉES

TIP

To save some time get the cauliflower, bacon and onion already chopped or maybe use cauliflower rice and pre-diced frozen bacon and onion all from a deli.

Cauliflower and Bacon Soup

INGREDIENTS

½ large cauliflower
3 bacon rashers, chopped
1 onion, diced
4 cups water
2 chicken stock cubes
⅓ cup cream
Parsley

METHOD

1. Mix bacon and onion together in a large saucepan and cook until the onion is soft.
2. Add the cauliflower, water and stock cubes. Bring to the boil, reduce heat and allow to simmer covered for 20 minutes until the cauliflower is tender.
3. Blend or process the soup until smooth.
4. Return the soup to the saucepan and bring to the boil. Add cream, parsley and heat through without boiling.

WHAT'S THE DIFFERENCE?

Believe it or not there are apparently 10 different types of flour for baking out there. I am just going to cover the 3 most common flours I use when cooking. I'm not a fancy cook so no fancy flours here!

Self-raising flour has baking powder and salt added to it. This flour is generally used for preparing sponge cakes, scones, muffins, etc.

Plain flour is sometimes referred to as an all-purpose flour. It does not have the baking powder and salt in it. This flour is generally used for biscuits, breads and pizza bases.

Gluten-free flour can include almond flour, coconut flour, hemp flour and so many others. These are suitable for people who are gluten sensitive.

I have tried cooking with both almond and coconut flour, but you need recipes specific to these flours— you can't just substitute.

WHAT'S THE DIFFERENCE?

Lemongrass brings its bright citrus and herbal notes to everything, from soups and marinades to salads and desserts.

Ginger packs tons of warm, pungent, peppery flavour that works well with meats and vegetables.

Garlic has long been a common seasoning worldwide, with a history of several thousand years of human consumption and use. Garlic has a strong, pungent smell and can be used in soups, dressings, virtually anything you want to add dept to. I add it to mash potatoes, potato bake and sometimes just roast whole cloves.

ENTRÉES

TIP

Cheerios could be used instead of Franks but are a little more fiddley

Frankfurt Snacks

INGREDIENTS

2 puff pastry sheets
4 Continental Frankfurt
1 egg
Your favourite sauce to serve

METHOD

1. *Slightly thaw the puff pastry.*
2. *Lightly beat the egg.*
3. *Cut pastry sheets in half, creating 4 rectangles.*
4. *Place the Frankfurt along one long edge of each pastry piece.*
5. *Brush the opposite edge with egg.*
6. *Roll the Frankfurt and pastry, then press egg edge to seal.*
7. *Brush rolls lightly with egg.*
8. *Cut each roll into 12.*
9. *Place pieces cut side up on an oven tray and bake at 200° for 10-12 minutes.*

WHAT'S THE DIFFERENCE?

Cherry tomatoes are much smaller than most other varieties, but they taste delicious. They are often used in salads and on skewers.

Field tomatoes are grown outside, without plastic coverings. They can and are started under cover but matured and ripened in the field.

WHAT'S THE DIFFERENCE?

Truss tomatoes continue to ripen and sweeten by keeping them on the vine, ensuring they are at their optimum when you are ready to use them.

Roma tomatoes tend to be oblong in shape and heavy for their size. They are used for both canning and producing tomato paste.

ENTRÉES

Carrot Salad

INGREDIENTS

6 medium carrots
½ cup shredded coconut
½ cup sultanas

METHOD

1. Peel and grate the carrots.
2. Wash and dry the sultanas.
3. Toss all of the ingredients together.

Make sure to use plump, soft sultanas. This sweet salad is delicious without dressing. To help save time, buy the carrot already grated.

ENTRÉES

TIP

Making tortilla chips:
1. Take 8 corn tortillas and cut them into quarters.
2. Place them as a single layer on a baking tray.
3. Bake at 180° in the oven until crisp.

Mini Nacho

INGREDIENTS

32 unsalted tortilla chips
½ cup grated cheese
300g jar salsa,
    pick your heat

METHOD

1. Preheat the grill to Hot.
2. Place tortilla chips in a single layer on a non-stick baking tray.
3. Top each chip with a spoonful of salsa.
4. Place a little cheese on top of each.
5. Place baking tray on the grill rack about 10cm from the grill. Grill until the cheese melts, about 1-2 minutes.
4. Serve while hot.

WHAT'S THE DIFFERENCE?

Canola oil comes from a variety of Rapeseed. It has a mild flavour and is great to use when you want to cook something on high heat or as a dressing if you don't want extra flavour.

Margarine is a processed food that is designed to taste and look like butter. You can use it instead of butter in recipes, but the taste and texture may change if the recipe asks for butter.

Olive oil - Extra-virgin oil comes from cold-pressed olives usually has a greenish colour and more smell.

Virgin/olive oil are blends of both cold-pressed and processed oils. They are often used in Mediterranean cooking.

WHAT'S THE DIFFERENCE?

Coconut Oil - Pure/virgin comes from pressing fresh coconut meat. It keeps the coconut smell and flavour.

Refined comes from dried coconuts and is processed filtering the coconut smell and flavour.

Sunflower oil is oil pressed from sunflower seeds. It has a light colour and mild flavour.

Butter is a dairy product made from milk or cream. It helps add moisture and flavour in cooking.

ENTRÉES

TIP

If you're not a fan of mint (like my daughter) try basil or parsley.

Seafood Watermelon Salad

INGREDIENTS

1kg cooked prawns
500g watermelon (seedless)
½ cup mint leaves
200g marinated feta
1 lemon, zested and juiced
2 tbsp olive oil or
  coconut oil
Pepper to taste

METHOD

1. *The cooked prawns should be peeled, deveined but the tails should be left on. Put to the side.*
2. *Remove the rind from the watermelon and slice thinly.*
3. *Crumble the feta into coarse crumbles.*
4. *Arrange prawns, watermelon, mint and feta on a serving plate.*
5. *Sprinkle with lemon zest.*
6. *Pour the lemon juice and oil over the top.*
7. *Sprinkle pepper to taste.*

TIP

To stop bowls and cutting boards from slipping on benches place a damp cloth under it.

Cauliflower Salad

INGREDIENTS

Traditional mayonnaise or garlic aioli
Curry powder, to taste
Cauliflower
Broccoli
Beans
Celery

METHOD

1. Pull apart the cauliflower and broccoli. Cut the beans into sections. Slice the celery.
2. Mix the mayonnaise and curry together to your desired taste.
3. Mix all the vegetables together.
4. Mix though the mayonnaise.

This is best made the day before. I love it with some bacon pieces.

WHAT'S THE DIFFERENCE?

Tray (sheet pan) has shallow sides and is usually the go-to for cooking in the oven. In my house we use it for cooking everything from biscuits to pizzas or roast potatoes

Loaf pan is usually 9" (24cm) long, 5" (14cm) wide and 2.6" (6cm) deep. It is a versatile pan for meatloaf, cakes or breads.

Springform has a removable outer edge that unclasps easily after baking. This pan is a must for baking or cold cheesecakes.

WHAT'S THE DIFFERENCE?

9" Round cake pan is the most popular pan for cooking cakes, and also comes 8". Ideal for making layered cakes.

Tart pan is for small pies or tarts. This is the one I use for the tart recipes that have a ready-made biscuit base you need to soften in the oven. It is shallower than a muffin tray.

Muffin/cupcake trays also come in mini sizes for fun bite-size treats. Most cake recipes can be used in a muffin tray by reducing the cook time as well as quiche mixes for kid's lunches

8" Square baking pan most bar and brownie recipes fit this size pan.

ENTRÉES

TIP

To make slicing avocado easier, slice it while it is still in the skin.

Beetroot Salad

INGREDIENTS

2 beetroot, cooked (not canned)
French dressing
Horseradish, grated

METHOD

1. *Slice the beetroot and arrange on a plate/bowl.*
2. *Sprinkle with the grated horseradish.*
3. *Splash the French dressing over everything*
4. *The beetroot can be bought already cooked in the veggie section of the supermarkets or you can buy raw and cook yourself.*

If you're like me and not a fan of horseradish, add a bit of any kind of mustard to the French dressing and leave the horseradish out.

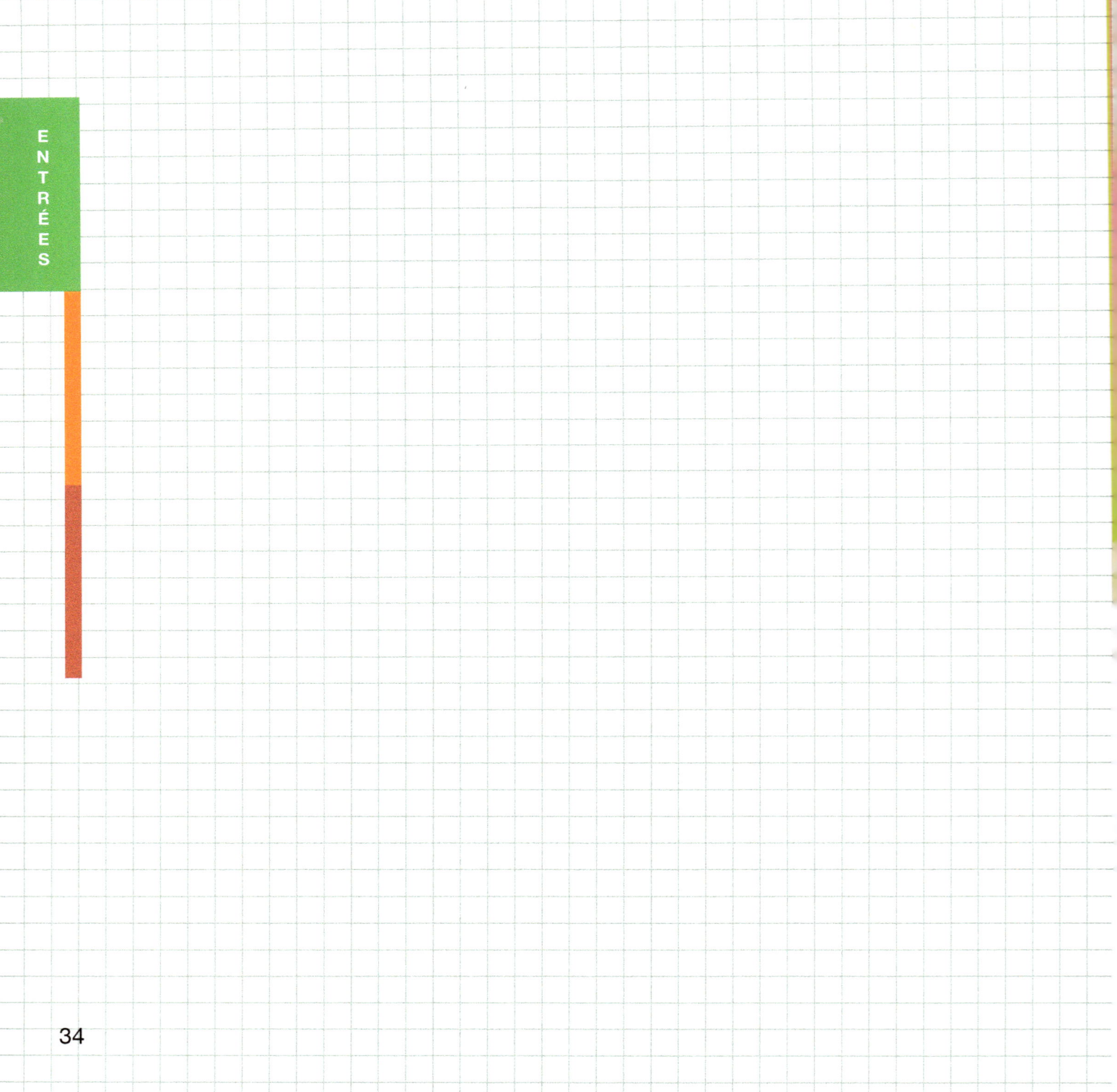

Cucumber Salad

INGREDIENTS

1 large cucumber
1 small onion
Salt
2 tsp lemon juice

INGREDIENTS

1. Peel the cucumber and scratch up (score) with a fork. Cut into thin slices.
2. Peel onion, cut into thin slices.
3. Sprinkle salt over cucumber and let stand for 30 minutes, then drain.
4. Mix cucumber, onion and lemon juice until well-combined.

You could add some herbs if you like. These quantities will work nicely as two side-dish serves

ENTRÉES

TIP

Use proper measuring cups and spoons while cooking. Proper measuring tools will make everything a lot easier. My Aunty is the only person I know who can cook by adding a bit of this and a bit of that.

Green Salad

INGREDIENTS

1 bunch celery
1 lettuce
1 capsicum (any colour)
1 large cucumber
½ cup sultanas

METHOD

1. Wash the lettuce and tear into small pieces.
2. Chop celery however you like.
3. Remove seeds and chop capsicum.
4. Cut cucumber into small pieces.
5. Wash and dry sultanas.
6. Toss everything together in a bowl, add dressing if you like.

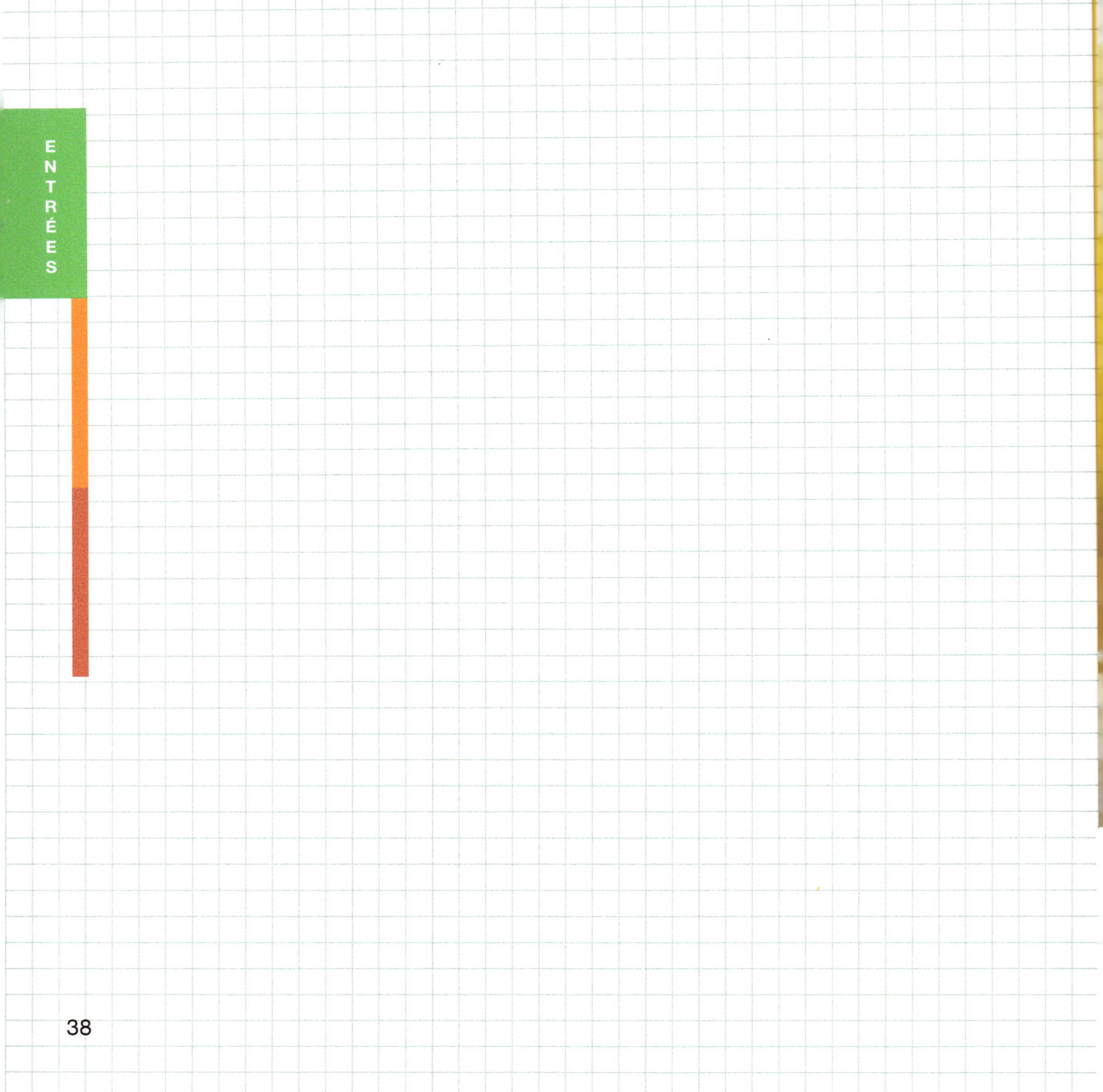

Minted Cucumber Salad

INGREDIENTS

1 small lettuce
1 small cucumber
3 tbsp mint, chopped
2 tbsp oil (olive or coconut oil)
2 tbsp white vinegar
½ tsp sugar
Pinch dry mustard

INGREDIENTS

1. Wash and dry the lettuce and tear into small pieces, place in a bowl.
2. Cut cucumber into very thin slices and place in the same bowl with the lettuce.
3. Put the mint, oil, vinegar, sugar, mustard, salt and pepper to taste into a jar with a lid and shake until all combined.
4. Pour dressing over the lettuce and cucumber toss and serve.

If you aren't a fan of mint swap it out for some basil or parsley.

Mains

The main course dishes

MAINS

Chicken Pasta Salad

INGREDIENTS

2 cups pasta twists, uncooked
1 carrot
1 red capsicum
2 zucchinis
2 shallots
2 cups cooked chicken, chopped
440g can corn kernels, drained

Dressing

¼ cup cream
¼ cup mayonnaise (I like whole egg)
½ cup Italian dressing

METHOD

1. Cut the carrot and the capsicum into thin strips. Slice the zucchini. Chop the shallots.
2. Cook pasta as directed.
3. In a large bowl combine pasta, carrots, capsicum, zucchinis, chicken, corn and shallots.
4. Just before serving, combine all dressing ingredients in another bowl and pour over pasta. Mix and combine well.

This can also be nice warm as a main. Put everything in a deep frypan and mix some pouring or cooking cream through, but leave the mayonnaise and dressing out. You could really use any pasta; add anything you like. I don't like capsicum, so I add mushrooms.

TIP

To find out if eggs are fresh, fill a basin with water and place the egg in the basin. A fresh egg will sink to the bottom, a bad egg will float.

Meatloaf (Bake or Microwave)

INGREDIENTS

750g mince
1 egg
½ packet dry tomato soup
¼ cup stale breadcrumbs
2 boiled eggs

METHOD

1. *Mix all the ingredients, except the boiled eggs.*
2. *Press half the mixture into a greased bar tin or microwave safe pan.*
3. *Layer the boiled eggs over the mixture.*
4. *Press in remaining mixture over the top of the boiled eggs.*
5. *Bake in a moderate oven for 1 hour or microwave on High for 20 minutes.*
6. *Let stand for 5 minutes, then turn onto a wire rack.*

MAINS

TIP

Get yourself a set of good quality knives and keep them sharp.

Microwave Apricot Chicken

INGREDIENTS

40g packet French onion soup
1kg chicken pieces
425g can apricot halves, drained
400g can of apricot nectar
1 tbsp cornflour

METHOD

1. Place chicken pieces in a round, shallow microwave dish.
2. Pour the French onion soup mix and ⅔ of a cup of the apricot nectar (reserve the remaining) over the chicken.
3. Cover and microwave on Medium High for 15-17 minutes.
4. Rotate the chicken pieces and add apricot halves.
5. Cook on Medium High for a further 8-10 minutes or until the chicken is cooked.
6. Combine the cornflour with the leftover apricot nectar and mix into the chicken immediately.
7. Allow to stand for 5 minutes before serving with rice.

If pushed for time, use one of the 90 second microwave rice pouches.

TIP

If you are going to use butter and it is a bit hard, use a grater and grate the butter for easy mixing into dough.

MAINS

Microwave Vegetable Risotto

INGREDIENTS

1 onion, diced
2 cups of assorted vegetables, chopped
60g butter
4 bacon rashers, diced
3 chicken or beef stock cubes
2 cups of boiling water
1 cup of long grain rice

METHOD

1. Place the onion, butter and bacon in a large casserole dish.
2. Cook 4-5 minutes on High. Stir well.
3. Dissolve the stock cubes in boiling water and add to the onion mixture.
4. Stir in the remaining ingredients, (vegies and rice).
5. Cover with the lid and cook for 20 minutes on High. Do not stir while cooking. At the end of cooking all the liquid will be absorbed.
6. Leave to stand for 5 minutes before serving.

Bacon and vegies can be bought already diced or even frozen. Jasmin rice is very nice in this recipe.

TIP

If beef mince is a bit dry for you, try a beef and pork mix. Minced pork is fattier.

Loaded Baked Potato

INGREDIENTS

1 large potato per person
Bacon, diced
Mushrooms, sliced
Coleslaw, readymade
Sour cream
Grated cheese

METHOD

1. *Preheat the oven to 200°, put the potatoes on an oven tray and cook for about 1 hour (check with a knife to make sure they are cooked all the way through).*
2. *Add the bacon and mushrooms to a fry pan and cook.*
3. *When the potatoes are cooked, put each potato on its own plate and cut into 4.*
4. *Then put the bacon/mushroom mix, coleslaw, sour cream and cheese in the middle of the table and let everyone load their own potato.*

For an adult, I usually get a potato the size of my hand. We sometimes add some grated or diced beetroot. To help save time the bacon and mushrooms can be bought already cut.

TIP

To help with smells in your microwave, try putting a small bowl of baking soda in there when not being used. It works for the fridge, just remember to take it out before cooking in it.

Easy Noodle Stirfry

INGREDIENTS

110g bowl of Suimin Red Beef Curry noodles
1 tbsp peanut oil
1 small onion
250g cooked BBQ chicken
1 carrot
1 cup baby spinach leaves
1 spring onion

METHOD

1. Peel and thinly slice the carrot. Chop the spring onion and the onion.
2. Prepare noodles as directed, using vegetable pouch but not the flavour pouch.
3. Drain the noodles, reserving ¼ cup of the stock.
4. Using a deep fry pan, heat the oil then add the onion and beef. Stir until the beef is cooked.
5. Add the flavour pouch, stir and cook for about 1 minute.
6. Add the carrot and spinach and fry while stirring for about 2 minutes. Add the noodles, the kept stock and spring onion.

Sometimes the red curry minute noodles are hard to find so just use some other flavour.

TIP

You can use an egg slicer to slice a lot of things. I have cut strawberries, kiwi fruit and mushrooms with an egg slicer.

Tuna Dish

INGREDIENTS

Onion
1 large tin tuna, drained
1 can cream of asparagus soup
½ cup milk
½-1 cup of cheese

METHOD

1. *Cook the onion in a large pan.*
2. *Make up the soup as directed on the can and add to the onion.*
3. *Add all the other ingredients, including the cheese, and stir until well mixed and heated through.*
4. *If you want to add vegies add a tin of your preferred choice, just make sure you drain it first before adding it to the mix.*

Serve with rice, pasta, salad or a par bake roll.

TIP

If you don't want your natural peanut butter separating, store the jar upside down.

Quick Casserole

INGREDIENTS

500g mince
2 tins vegetable soup

METHOD

1. Brown the mince in a fry pan with a little oil.
2. Place the mince into the casserole dish.
3. Add the 2 tins of vegetable soup and stir.
4. Cook in the oven at 200° for 40 minutes.

This is great with rice, or the bake at home rolls. For something a bit different, you can put the mix into small ramekins and cook with some puff pastry over the top or mashed potato for pies.

TIP

If serving salad, meat or seafood put some ice in a zip lock bag then put the bagged ice in a bowl. Cover with lettuce or kale for decoration to cover the bag.

MAINS

Smoked Cod Casserole

INGREDIENTS

500g of smoked cod
1 cup water
½ cup corn kernels
Parsley to taste, chopped
1 packet potato and leek soup
1 cup milk
½ cup capsicum, diced
½ cup grated cheese
½ cup peas

METHOD

1. Cut cod into chunky 2.5cm pieces. Cover with water and boil for 3 minutes, drain and set aside.
2. In the same saucepan add the packet soup, milk and water and simmer for 5 minutes.
3. Mix through the corn, capsicum, cheese, peas and parsley.
4. Add fish and reheat gently.

You can use other vegetables or a different firm fish.

WHAT'S THE DIFFERENCE?

Iceberg is a variety of lettuce that grows in a round head and looks a bit like a cabbage.

Oak leaf lettuce gets its name from the shape of its leaves, as they resemble oak tree leaves. This lettuce can come in green or red.

Mignonette lettuce has soft curly leaves with a small heart. This is one of the most common lettuce for home gardeners.

WHAT'S THE DIFFERENCE?

Rocket has individual leaves with a mild peppery taste, and is very popular in salads.

Coral grows into medium large head size, bright green or red/green leaves and are tender in taste and some say taste a little bitter. This one is also popular with home gardeners. *This is the one I grow and is very easy.*

MAINS

Sausage Stew

INGREDIENTS

Sausages (beef or pork)
1½ cups of potato, cubed
1½ cups of carrot, cubed
1 cup peas
1 packet tomato soup

METHOD

1. Cook sausages and cut each into 3-4 pieces.
2. Boil potatoes and carrots until tender.
3. Add the peas.
4. Add tomato soup to the simmering vegetables and stir.
5. Add sausages and simmer gently until sausages are reheated.

A lot of the vegetables can be bought pre-cut or frozen. If tomato soup is not for you, it can be made with 3 tbsp of gravy mix instead.

MAINS

TIP

You can freeze leftover cooked pasta by coating the pasta with olive oil. Put into zip lock freezer bags or containers. It will last about 3 months in the freezer. Just reheat when needed. But if your pasta is overcooked don't bother because you will probably end up with mush when you try to reheat.

10-minute Tuna

INGREDIENTS

425g tin of tuna, drained
1 stick of celery
1 cup evaporated milk
4 cups uncooked pasta shells
1 green capsicum
1 can mushroom soup
1 tbsp flour
1 onion

METHOD

1. Chop the onion and the celery.
2. Cook pasta as directed.
3. Cook onion and capsicum in a little oil until soft.
4. Add flour and while stirring cook for 1 minute.
5. Gradually stir in the evaporated milk, then the mushroom soup.
6. Cook but do not boil.
7. Add drained tuna and celery and cook for 5 minutes.
8. Stir through pasta.

If you like, add a handful of peas.

TIP

Adding a pinch of baking soda when cooking onions will reduce cooking time and quicken browning.

Rice with Seafood

INGREDIENTS

100g seafood mix
   (marinara mix)
1 onion
6 shallots
2 tbsp oil
2 eggs
1½ cups long grain rice
1 tbsp soy sauce

METHOD

1. Peel onion and cut into thin slices. Chop shallots.
2. Cook rice as per instructions.
3. Heat oil in a large pan and add onion. Cook until soft.
4. Beat eggs and add to the pan with onions. Stir lightly and cook until egg is set.
5. Remove and cut omelette into large pieces.
6. In the same large pan cook the seafood, then add the cooked rice and mix well. Add chopped shallots and continue cooking until all heated through.
7. When cooked, put on a plate or bowl and place omelette pieces on top. You can add some chilli if you want some heat.

WHAT'S THE DIFFERENCE?

Button Mushrooms are also called baby mushrooms or white mushrooms. Button mushrooms are the ones you usually find at the grocery store and are by far the most common type of mushroom. They are used in a variety of cooking including pizzas, spaghetti etc.

Portobello mushrooms are much larger than most other mushrooms and have a fleshier texture. They have their cap completely open. These mushrooms are usually the ones used as vegetarian burgers or stuffed with other ingredients.

Shitake mushrooms are commonly used in Asian cooking and commonly sold dried. Shiitake mushrooms have a texture similar to portobellos.

WHAT'S THE DIFFERENCE?

Silverbeet is part of the, believe it or not, beet family. It has large bunches of bright-green, thick leaves that have a deep earthy flavour and a wonderful bitter sweetness.

Spinach is a leafy dark green with spoon-shaped leaves. Depending upon variety and maturity, baby spinach can be sweet and as the plant matures becomes earthy, nutty and even tangy.

TIP

Coat your cheese grater with non-stick spray for easy grating.

MAINS

Quickest Chicken Curry

INGREDIENTS

1.3kg cooked chicken
¼ cup peanut oil
⅓ cup red curry paste
400ml can coconut milk
¼ cup fish sauce
2 tbsp sugar
½ cup crunchy peanut paste

METHOD

1. Heat oil in large saucepan, add curry paste and stir over heat for 1 minute.
2. Stir in coconut milk, fish sauce, sugar and peanut paste. Cook over Medium heat until the mixture boils and thickens.
3. Add chicken, stir through and heat for about 5 minutes or until the mixture is hot.

If you like a little more heat add chilli to taste. Serve with rice if you like.

MAINS

Spinach, Ham and Tomato Bake

INGREDIENTS

250g ham
2 cups baby spinach
1 punnet cherry tomatoes
4 spring onions
3 eggs
300ml thickened cream
⅓ cup milk
½ tsp paprika
1½ cups grated cheese

METHOD

1. Preheat the oven to 180°. Lightly grease a 4-cup baking dish.
2. Roughly chop spinach, halve the tomatoes, dice the ham and chop the white part of the spring onion. Place in the baking dish and stir.
3. In a separate jug/bowl, whisk the eggs then mix in the cream and milk. Add the spice you are using and 1 cup of the grated cheese.
4. Pour over spinach and tomatoes, and sprinkle the top with the remaining cheese.
5. Bake for 30 minutes or until set. Garnish with some of the tops of the spring onions.

If you like heat, replace the paprika with chilli powder.

MAINS

Omelettes On-the-Go

INGREDIENTS

8 bread slices
6 eggs
¼ cup milk or water
Some dried herbs
2 rashers bacon, chopped

INGREDIENTS

1. Butter each slice of bread on both sides then remove the centre of each slice.
2. Beat the eggs and milk/water together, then add herbs and bacon.
3. Place the bread slices into a frying pan and spoon a little of the egg mixture into the centre.
4. When the egg is nearly set, turn over and cook the other side.

You can cheat and use the pre-diced bacon from the shop. We used to do this for camping and it can be good for getting rid of slightly stale bread.

MAINS

TIP

Crack eggs on a flat surface instead of the edge of a bowl.

Fettuccini Chicken

Serves 4

INGREDIENTS

1 cup cooked chicken
500g fettuccini pasta
420g cream of chicken
  condensed soup

METHOD

1. *Cook fettuccini according to instructions.*
2. *Drain excess water.*
3. *Make up the soup cold but as directed.*
4. *Add chicken and soup to the pasta and heat through.*

Cheat and grab a roast chicken from Coles or Woolworths. I usually add a handful of peas, but you could add some cooked mushrooms or other cooked vegetable if you like.

MAINS

MAINS

TIP

Try using a pizza cutter for cutting herbs.

Sausage Salad

INGREDIENTS

500g Italian pork sausages
400g can chickpeas, rinsed and drained
350g mixed medley tomatoes, halved
120g baby spinach
1 small red onion
190g jar basil pesto

METHOD

1. Cook the sausages either on the stove or BBQ.
2. When cooked, thickly slice diagonally.
3. Place the sausage, chickpeas, tomato, baby spinach and half the pesto in a large bowl and combine gently.
4. Arrange on a serving plate.
5. Drizzle the remaining pesto over the top.

You could mix it up by using 250g chorizo and 250g pork sausage. I have used as a salad for four people but it is nice as a main for two people as well.

WHAT'S THE DIFFERENCE?

Onions, who would have thought there were so many, and each is ideal for a certain type of cooking.

White onion has a sweeter, milder flavour. It can be used raw in salsa and stir-fry.

Red onion has the mildest flavour, more often used raw, especially in salads. It is great in guacamole and bruschetta. Perfect for pickling.

WHAT'S THE DIFFERENCE?

Yellow onion has the deepest flavour and is best used in cooking. It is great in soups and sauces or gravy for bangers and mash.

Sweet onion has a sweeter flavour and is good for frying or roasting with other vegetables. They are generally smaller than yellow onions.

Spring onion usually used as a raw garnish and topping.

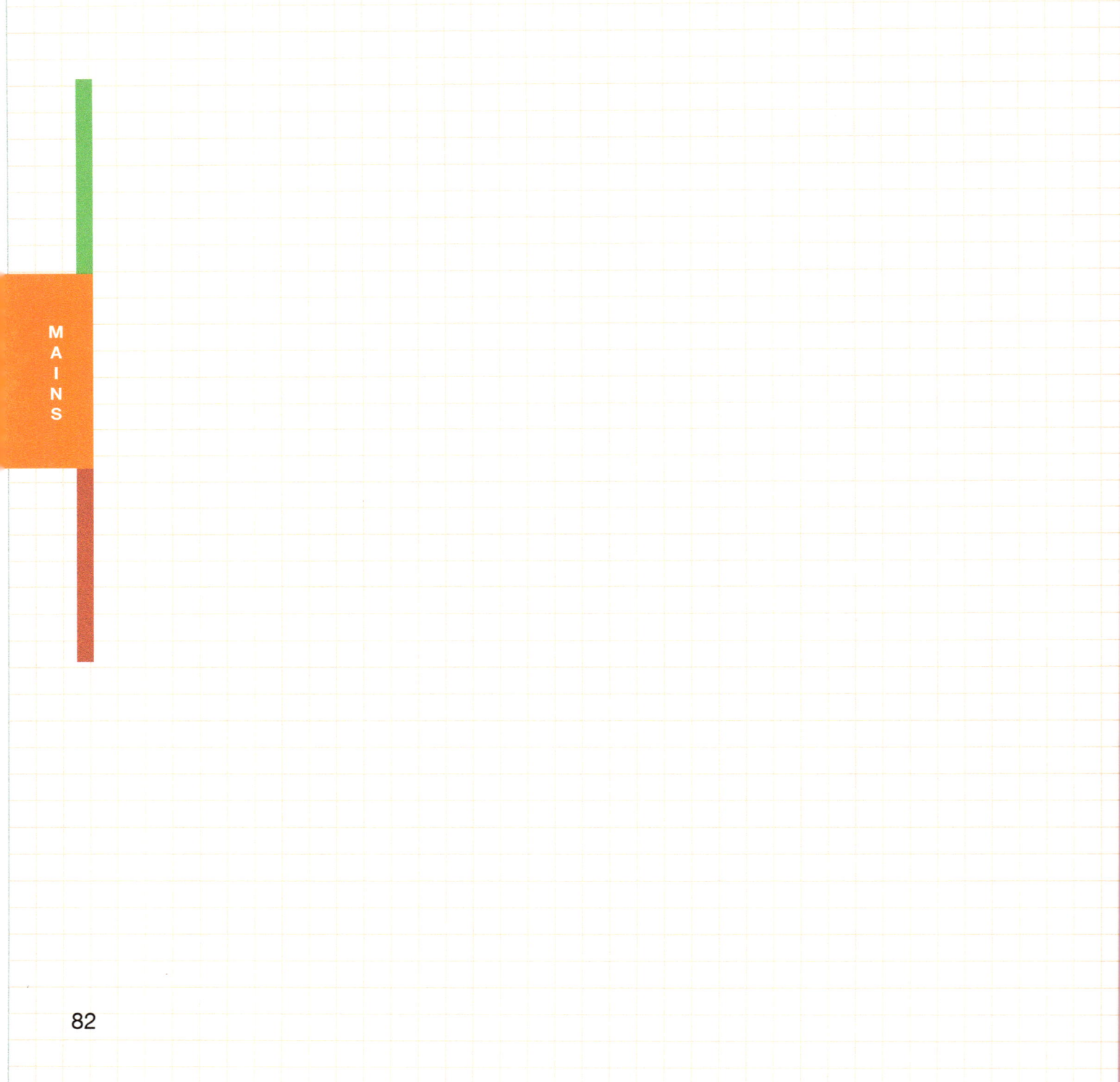

MAINS

Macaroni Bake

INGREDIENTS

1½ cups small macaroni, cooked
4 bacon rashers
1 onion, diced
½ cup milk
440g tin tomato soup
1 cup grated cheese

METHOD

1. Put macaroni in an 8-cup casserole dish.
2. Fry bacon and onion until cooked, then stir into macaroni.
3. Stir in soup, milk and cheese.
4. Bake at 190° for 45 minutes.

I know this is pasta, but it is a kids favourite. This is an easy and inexpensive recipe to alter if you have more people to feed.

TIP

Freeze ginger in a plastic container or resealable bag.

MAINS

Hawaiian Mini Pizzas

INGREDIENTS

100g shredded ham
225g pineapple pieces, drained
1 cup cheese
125g can creamed corn
12 dinner rolls, halved

METHOD

1. Combine ham, pineapple, cheese and corn in a bowl.
2. Place roll halves on an oven tray and spread with ham mixture.
3. Bake rolls at 200° for about 10 minutes until the cheese is melted and rolls are crispy.
4. Serve warm.

These are great if you are trying to feed a lot of kids quickly.
The mixture can be made up to an hour before you need it, letting you get a head start.

TIP

Use uncooked instant potato for thickening stews, soups and gravies. Add a little at a time until the desired consistency is obtained.

MAINS

Asparagus Dish

INGREDIENTS

1 cup SAO cracker crumbs
1 egg
1 tin asparagus tips
1 cup asparagus liquid
Cheese

METHOD

1. Mix all the ingredients together except the cheese.
2. Put in a pie dish and sprinkle with cheese.
3. Cook in a Moderate oven for 15 minutes.

If you don't have a full cup of asparagus liquid, top up with milk.

WHAT'S THE DIFFERENCE?

Did you know black peppercorns are just green peppercorns that have been cooked and dried out?

Whole pepper corns work only if the dish is to be cooked enough to soften the corns, so ideally it is used in soups and meatloaf, casserole or stew. While eating you will eventually bite into one, giving a burst of peppery flavour. I use these when cooking silverside.

Cracked pepper corns have a stronger peppery flavour than ground black pepper. The texture with cracked black pepper offers a crunchier texture than ground black pepper.

Ground black pepper is more of an all-purpose spice good for sauces and other smooth, mildly-flavoured dishes. If you are making a dish where a smooth texture is key or where you need the spice to mix evenly.

WHAT'S THE DIFFERENCE?

Balsamic vinegar is cooked grapes. It is best for marinades, sauces and salads. It is a little sweeter and has a rich flavour.

Wine vinegar is either made from fermented red or white wine. Red wine vinegar is generally used for pickling, deglazing pans, marinating meats, making sauces and is found in certain desserts. White wine vinegar is used to make Hollandaise and Béarnaise sauces, vinaigrettes, soups, and stews.

Apple cider vinegar is made from fermented apple cider. It has been reported to provide many health benefits.

Rice vinegar is made from fermented rice. It has a milder flavour and is generally used in Asian cooking.

White vinegar is made from fermented alcohol with water added, and is mildly acidic. It is a general use vinegar and can be used in most cooking. White vinegar has become an alternative for chemical free cleaning.

MAINS

Chicken and Corn Casserole

INGREDIENTS

1 BBQ chicken
1 tin cream of chicken and corn soup
270g can corn kernels, drained

INGREDIENTS

1. *Make up the soup cold, but as directed.*
2. *Break chicken in pieces, remove the skin and the bones for convenience.*
3. *Place chicken in a casserole dish.*
4. *Mix corn and soup together and pour over the chicken.*
5. *Cover and cook at 200° for about 30 minutes.*

You can use asparagus pieces instead of corn if you like.

TIP

Remember raw rice triples when cooked, so if a recipe needs 1 cup of cooked rice, use ⅓ cup raw rice.

Savoury Chicken Noodle

INGREDIENTS

1 packet chicken noodle soup
450g mince
¾ cup uncooked rice
1 medium onion, chopped
600ml water
Salt and pepper to taste

METHOD

1. Combine all of the ingredients in a casserole dish and cover.
2. Cook in the oven at 200° for 1 hour.

You can substitute the mince with red lentils if you prefer. You can throw a handful of vegies like peas, beans, capsicum or even some chilli in before cooking for colour if you like.

TIP

An easy way to rinse uncooked rice is place the rice in a clean Chux cloth and hold under running water, moving the rice around carefully.

Savoury Pie

INGREDIENTS

3 eggs
1¾ cups milk
¼ cup plain flour
½ cup shallots, chopped
½ cup ham, chopped
½ cup grated cheese

METHOD

1. Place all of the ingredients in a bowl and mix well.
2. Pour the mixture into a deep 1.5L microwave-safe dish.
3. Microwave for 15 minutes or cook in the oven at 180° for 60 minutes.

To help save time and washing up, I mix and cook in a deep-sided casserole dish. This easy pie also comes in a sweet alternative, (see Impossible Pie on page 149). This is nice served hot or cold for a quick, easy dinner or something special to take on a picnic.

TIP

If you have forgotten to remove butter from the fridge before cooking, save time by peeling off slices with a vegetable peeler.

Lamb Stew

INGREDIENTS

4 lamb forequarter chops, halved
1½ cup soup mix
3 cups frozen vegetables
1½ litres of hot water
3 tbsp tomato sauce
3 tbsp soy sauce
3 tbsp oyster sauce
1 stock cube

METHOD

1. *Place all of the ingredients into a large, heavy base pot.*
2. *Bring to boil and stir intermittently.*
3. *Simmer until tender.*
4. *Serve with rice or bread.*

If you don't want to use frozen vegetables, you can use 2 carrots, 2 potatoes and 1 onion. This is also an easy recipe for camping and cooking in a camp oven.

MAINS

Meatloaf

INGREDIENTS

500g mince
1 cup rice bubbles
  or rolled oats
2 tbsp butter, melted
1 cup milk
2 bacon slices
Salt and pepper to taste

METHOD

1. Combine all the ingredients, except the bacon.
2. Push into a loaf tin.
3. Lay slices of bacon across the top.
4. Bake in the oven at 200° for 2 hours.

Can serve hot or cold.

TIP

There are a lot of variables but roughly jelly is partially set after 30–60 minutes in the fridge but keep your eye on it and use your best judgement.

Kids Casserole

INGREDIENTS

500g Cheerios
½ cup grated cheese
1 cup instant milk powder
450g can tomato soup

METHOD

1. *Combine all of the ingredients in a saucepan.*
2. *Bring to the boil and stir.*
3. *Simmer gently for 5 minutes.*

TIP

To reduce waste, organise your fridge and pantry by placing the soonest use-by dates towards the front and rotating stuff so that shorter shelf-life items or items nearing their use-by date get used first.

Ham and Vege Egg Pie

INGREDIENTS

5-6 slices of ham
1½ cups carrot, grated
1½ cups zucchini, grated
1 packet chicken supreme soup
6 eggs
1 cup milk

METHOD

1. Line a 23cm greased quiche dish with the ham slices.
2. Spread grated carrot and zucchini evenly over the ham.
3. Whisk together soup mix, eggs and milk.
4. Pour gently over the vegetables.
5. Bake at 180° for 30-35 minutes or until the egg mixture is set and golden brown.

This is nice hot or cold.

TIP

Most recipes can be altered slightly, which can help with shopping for what is in season and therefore help save money.

Baked Bean Hash

INGREDIENTS

6 hash brown, frozen
425g can baked beans
4 eggs
2 bacon rashers, chopped
Some dried herbs
  or fresh parsley

METHOD

1. *Place the frozen hash browns in the bottom of a baking dish.*
2. *Pour baked beans over the top of hash browns.*
3. *Beat the eggs, then mix in bacon and any herbs.*
4. *Pour the egg mixture over baked beans.*
5. *Bake at 190° until the egg is set (roughly 35-40 minutes).*

As a cheat, you can use diced bacon from the deli.

TIP

Try sweetening cream with honey—it stays firmer and keeps whipped longer.

MAINS

Chicken and Spinach Risotto

INGREDIENTS

1 tbsp oil
1 onion
4 chicken thigh fillets
2 cups Arborio rice
420g can condensed creamy creamy chicken soup
3¼ cups chicken stock
2 spinach leaves
½ cup finely grated parmesan cheese

INGREDIENTS

1. Peel and dice the onion. Chop the spinach leaves. Finely dice the chicken (if not pre-cut).
2. Heat the oil in a large, lidded saucepan. Add the chicken and onion, and cook until the onion has softened.
3. Add rice and toss to coat, then add the stock and soup. Stir to mix well.
4. Cover and gently simmer for 25 minutes, stirring occasionally until the rice is cooked and water has been absorbed.
5. Stir in the spinach and parmesan cheese. Let sit for 2 minutes and then serve.

You can buy the chicken already diced or as stir-fry strips. Use water instead of the chicken stock if you prefer. For something different, add a handful of mushrooms as well when cooking the chicken and onion.

Desserts

Sweets and Snacks

DESSERTS

Peanut Butter Biscuits

INGREDIENTS

4 cups rice cereal
   (Rice Bubbles or similar)
2 tbsp peanut butter
200g condensed milk

METHOD

1. Mix all the ingredients together.
2. Using tablespoons, measure out portions on a foil-lined tray.
3. Bake on the centre shelf at 160° for 10 minutes.

You can substitute Nutella for the peanut butter. Make sure to check for any nut allergies before serving if using peanut butter.

WHAT'S THE DIFFERENCE?

White sugar or granulated sugar is the most common sugar used for cooking.

Caster sugar is just superfine sugar but not powdery like icing sugar. It is ideal in recipes where the sugar needs to fully dissolve, so it is often used in cakes or meringues. You can substitute other sugars if the final texture is not important.

Icing sugar is granulated sugar that has been finely ground to a soft powder. It is used for frostings and dusting.

WHAT'S THE DIFFERENCE?

Raw sugar is a granulated sugar that has a little molasses in it. You can substitute for both brown and white sugar but it is courser so the final texture could be a little different.

Brown Sugar is white sugar that has had cane molasses added. It is used to make biscuits soft and chewy.

DESSERTS

Baked Rice Pudding

INGREDIENTS

⅔ cup white rice
2 cups milk
1½ cups water
⅓ cup sugar
1 tbsp butter
1 tsp vanilla

METHOD

1. Rinse the rice and place in a greased casserole dish.
2. Add the other ingredients and mix with the rice.
3. Bake at 160° for 1½ hours or until rice is cooked, stirring occasionally.

I have also added at separate times for a different taste either some sultanas, pineapple pieces or shredded coconut.

TIP

What you need to know about simmering:
Slow Simmer *is when a couple of tiny bubbles erupt every 1 or 2 seconds.*
Simmer *happens when larger pockets of small, continuous bubbles erupt at the surface, displaying wisps of steam, with larger bubbles beginning to show.*
Rapid Simmer *is sometimes referred to as a gentle boil; it's mostly used to thicken liquid into sauce.*

Apricot Dessert

INGREDIENTS

825g can apricot halves
¾ cup sugar
2 level tbsp flour
300g carton sour cream
2 eggs
1 tsp vanilla
Cinnamon sugar

METHOD

1. Place apricot halves in the base of a 1.25L oven-proof dish.
2. Lightly beat the eggs.
3. Combine sugar, flour, sour cream, eggs and vanilla in a bowl.
4. Pour the mixture over the apricots.
5. Sprinkle with cinnamon sugar.
6. Cook on 210° for 15 minutes or until the egg mixture is set.
7. This can be served warm or cold.

You can substitute the apricot with plum halves instead. If a thinner dessert is preferred, reduce the flour to 2 dessertspoons. To make it easier, buy the cinnamon sugar from the store.

TIP

Blind baking means baking the crust without a filling. You would do this if you going to use an unbaked filling. To stop the pastry from puffing up in the middle before baking put some baking paper on it and put some weight on the centre while baking. You can get fancy pie weights, but usually I just use another baking dish.

Baked Lemon Pudding

INGREDIENTS

½ cup sugar
1 tbsp butter
2 tbsp flour
1 lemon, for juice and grated rind
1 cup milk
2 eggs

METHOD

1. Separate the egg yolk from the egg whites.
2. Beat the yolk well.
3. Beat the whites separately until stiff.
4. Mix the butter and sugar together until it has a creamy texture.
5. Add flour, lemon juice and rind, milk and egg yolk. Mix well.
6. Fold the beaten egg whites into the mixture.
7. Pour into a pie dish.
8. Sit in a dish of water in the oven and cook at 160° for 1½ hours.

TIP

Meal planning and shopping to meal plan can help save time and money.

DESSERTS

Apple Crumble

INGREDIENTS

1 can apple pie filling
½ cup soft butter
¾ cup brown sugar
1 cup plain flour

METHOD

1. Measure out 2 tbsp of butter and set aside.
2. Place apple filling into a baking dish.
3. Sprinkle with 2 tbsp of the brown sugar.
4. Mix the flour, the remaining butter and the remaining brown sugar in a bowl with your fingers until crumbly.
5. Sprinkle this over the top of the apple filling.
6. Melt the reserved 2 tbsp of butter and drizzle over the top.
7. Bake at 200° for 30 minutes, until the crumble is golden.

You can used other canned fruit like cherries or apricots or make your own stewed rhubarb.

WHAT'S THE DIFFERENCE?

There are four basic types of pastry, these are shortcrust pastry, filo pastry, choux pastry and puff pastry.

Puff pastry is a flaky, light pastry made by repeatedly folding and rolling out the pastry before baking.

Short crust pastry is a pastry often used for the base of tarts, quiches or pies. This pastry can be used to make both sweet and savory pies.

WHAT'S THE DIFFERENCE?

Filo pastry is tissue-thin sheets of pastry which need to be brushed with oil or melted butter before cooking. It can be used in many ways to wrap or roll fillings which can be either sweet or savoury, like Baklava and sausage rolls.

Choux pastry is a twice-cooked delicate French pastry typically eaten cold. The dough is used to make eclairs, buns, cream puffs and profiteroles.

DESSERTS

Barbequed Banana

INGREDIENTS

1 banana per person, skin on
Maple syrup

METHOD

1. Put a slit in each banana and drizzle some maple syrup onto the banana inside the skin.
2. Grill until hot with the slit facing up.
3. Pull the skin off and place on a plate or in a bowl (be careful as the banana and syrup will be hot) or eat straight out of the skin.
4. Serve with more maple syrup and ice-cream.

Pineapple could be used instead of banana if you like, and honey instead of maple syrup. You will need to take the skin off if using fresh pineapple. We did this camping, just wrap the banana in foil.

DESSERTS

TIP

When the jam jar is almost empty, add some olive oil, vinegar and any other desired seasoning and shake it well. It makes a good salad dressing.

DESSERTS

Custard Tart

INGREDIENTS

½ cup vanilla custard
1 tbsp double cream
6 sweet pastry shells

METHOD

1. *Mix the custard and cream together until there are no lumps.*
2. *Fill shells with custard mixture.*
3. *Top with whatever you like. You can use chocolate pieces or marshmallows or pieces of fruit.*
4. *Put in the fridge for at least 10 minutes and serve chilled.*

DESSERTS

TIP

Freshen up stale biscuits by placing a piece of bread in your biscuit container.

DESSERTS

Caramel Gingernuts

INGREDIENTS

1 packet gingernut biscuit
1 tin Nestle Top & Fill caramel

METHOD

1. Place biscuits in a patty pan/tart baking tray, 1 biscuit per hole.
2. Soften in a Cool oven (120°) for about 10 minutes.
3. Remove from the oven. The biscuit should have sunk into the hole if not just gently push down while warm.
4. Spoon Top & Fill into the biscuit moulds.
5. These can be decorated with cream, 100s & 1000s or whatever you like.

Perfect for any event! Try and eat just one, no one I know can.

WHAT'S THE DIFFERENCE?

Ice Cream to be classed as ice cream it is required to contain at least 10% milkfat (which is exactly that: fat from milk). It must also get churned during freezing, and sweetened usually with some kind of syrup.

Gelato means "ice cream" in Italian. But the two are a little different. Gelato contains less milk fat and less air churned into it during freezing, which makes its texture denser. Gelato is traditionally served at a slightly warmer temperature than ice cream, it feels a bit softer and looks glossier.

WHAT'S THE DIFFERENCE?

Frozen yoghurt uses, you guessed it, yoghurt instead of milk or cream giving this dairy dessert its creaminess. But other than that, it's made the same way as ice cream.

Sorbet contains no dairy and just has fruit and sugar. It's often churned in an ice cream maker, which makes it scoopable. Because of its refreshing fruit flavours restaurants sometimes use sorbet as a palette cleanser. It is easy to make at home.

DESSERTS

Peach Custard

INGREDIENTS

Jam filled Swiss Roll cake
Vanilla custard
1 can peach halves in syrup

METHOD

1. Cut cake into pieces and arrange on the bottom of a pie plate.
2. Place peach halves around and on top of the cake.
3. Pour a little of the peach syrup over the cake and add the peaches.
4. Pour custard over the cake and peaches until covered.
5. Chill and serve.

TIP

If you need to do a lot of prep, rather than walking to and from the bin or putting the scraps in the sink, get a large bowl and put all the scraps in the bowl and then make the one trip to the bin.

Custard Pie

INGREDIENTS

Frozen Short Crust Pastry or
   pre-prepared pie case
2 eggs
1 cup milk
1-2 tbsp sugar
Sprinkle of Nutmeg

METHOD

1. *Blind bake the pastry as per instructions (see pg 118 for tips on blind baking).*
2. *Beat together the eggs, milk and sugar*
3. *Gently pour the mixture into the pastry base.*
4. *Sprinkle with Nutmeg.*
5. *Cook in 220° oven for 10 minutes, then 180° for 30 minutes or until the custard has set.*

DESSERTS

TIP

To help prevent waste from old bread, put it in a processor and turn it into breadcrumbs. Put it in an airtight container and pop it in the freezer.

Jam Tarts

INGREDIENTS

275g packet frozen sweet tart cases
½ cup marmalade jam
1 orange for zest

METHOD

1. Place tart cases onto a baking tray, blind bake as per instructions (see page 118 for tips on blind baking). Spoon marmalade jam into tarts while there still warm.
2. Top with orange zest and a bit of cream if you like.

Like in the Caramel Gingernut recipe, try using a biscuit like an ANZAC biscuit for the base. Really you could use any jam for these tarts and top with what you like.

TIP

To help with avoiding impulse buying when shopping, try shopping online as this way you can track your spending as well.

DESSERTS

Biscuit Trifle

INGREDIENTS

2 packets raspberry jelly
250g packet Tiny Teddy biscuits
36 marshmallows, quartered

METHOD

1. *Make up jelly as directed on the packet. Place into the refrigerator and chill for about 3 hours or until lightly set (wobbly).*
2. *Using 6 250ml glasses, pour ⅓ of a cup of jelly into the bottom of each cup. Top with 8 biscuits, 6 marshmallows and again with another 8 biscuits.*
3. *Top glasses with another ⅓ cup of jelly. Top with a few more marshmallows and biscuits.*
4. *Refrigerate until ready to serve.*

You can use any flavoured jelly or even make a more adult tasting trifle using port wine jelly and some other small, sweet biscuits.

TIP

If you need to measure sticky syrups, sauces or honey, run the spoon under hot water first.

DESSERTS

Fruit Cake

INGREDIENTS

2 cups self-raising flour
1kg mixed fruit
300ml chocolate milk

METHOD

1. Soak the fruit in milk.
2. Sift the flour.
3. Mix together the flour, and milk-fruit mixture.
4. Pour into a greased or paper-lined 20cm round baking tin.
5. Cook at 200° for 1½ hours or until cooked (when tested the knife should come out clean).

My aunty has also cooked this using 500ml of fresh orange juice instead of the chocolate milk. This is a heavy, dense cake.

TIP

To help prevent salt from becoming sticky in humid or damp conditions add a couple of grains of rice into the salt. It will help absorb the moisture.

Sweet Jaffle

INGREDIENTS

8 slices white bread
125g spreadable cream cheese
1 cup frozen mixed berries
100g white chocolate melts, chopped
50g butter
½ cup maple syrup

METHOD

1. Preheat a sandwich press/jaffle maker.
2. Place the bread on a clean board and spread with cream cheese.
3. Top 4 bread slices with berries and sprinkle with chocolate.
4. Top with the other bread slices, cream cheese side down.
5. Spread the top of each sandwich with butter.
6. Cook in sandwich press until brown. The chocolate should be melted and the berries hot.
5. Dust with icing sugar and drizzle maple syrup over to serve.

Try strawberries and milk chocolate

TIP

To stop baking paper curling or moving when trying to cook, wipe it with a damp cloth and then place your baking paper on top.

DESSERTS

Christmas Logs

INGREDIENTS

1 banana
Peanut butter
Coconut

METHOD

1. *Cut the banana into 3 pieces.*
2. *Spread the peanut butter all over the banana.*
3. *Roll in coconut.*

You can substitute peanut butter for Nutella. Make sure to check for any nut allergies before serving.

TIP

For easy removal of pumpkin seeds use a metal ice-cream scoop and any large metal spoon.

Sugar Pastries

INGREDIENTS

Puff pastry sheets
Castor sugar

METHOD

1. Thaw the puff pastry.
2. Cover a board or your bench with castor sugar.
3. Place the puff pastry on the sugar.
4. Sprinkle the top of the pastry with more castor sugar
5. Roll each side up until they meet in the middle.
6. Cut the rolled pastry into 2.5cm pieces.
7. Place the pieces on a baking tray, allowing space for cooking.
8. Cook in a 230° oven for about 10 minutes or until golden brown.

TIP

To help keep a crunchy crust on reheated pizza, put a cup of water in the oven with the pizza.

DESSERTS

Impossible Pie

INGREDIENTS

3 eggs
1¾ cups milk
1 cup castor sugar
1 cup desiccated coconut
½ cup plain flour
125g melted butter

METHOD

1. Place all the ingredients in a bowl and beat well.
2. Pour the mixture into a deep 1.5L oven-proof pie dish.
3. Cook on 180° for approximately 60 minutes.

125g of butter was in the original recipe, however I can make this with only 90g. This easy pie also comes in a savoury alternative (see Savoury Pie on page 95). This is nice served hot or cold. My guys will cut bits off and eat straight from the fridge or pull the coconut top off while cooling.

DESSERTS

TIP

For the perfectly shaped poached egg, stir/swirl the near-boiling water with a spoon and place the egg into the middle.

Jelly Tart

INGREDIENTS

6 small pie shells
1 packet red jelly
1 cup water
1½ tsp corn flour
300ml cream

METHOD

1. Place the jelly crystals in the water and bring to the boil.
2. Blend the corn flour with a little cold water and add to the jelly mixture.
3. Stir until thick.
4. Allow to cool.
5. Place in a cooked pie shell and top with whipped cream.

TIP

To help stop your ice-cream cone from dripping, pop a small marshmallow in the bottom first and then the ice cream.

DESSERTS

Coconut Macaroons

INGREDIENTS

2 eggs
¾ cup sugar
3 cups coconut
Pinch of salt

METHOD

1. Separate the yolks from the egg whites.
2. Beat egg whites and salt until soft peaks form.
3. Beat egg yolks one at a time.
4. Gradually add sugar to yolks, making sure to beat until the sugar is dissolved.
5. Stir in the coconut and mix well.
6. Spoon tablespoonfuls of mixture on to an aluminium foil-lined tray.
7. Bake at 170° for 15–20 minutes or until golden brown.
8. Cool on the tray before serving.

TIP

If you are someone whose cupcakes need to be all the same try using an ice cream scoop to make the portions consistent.

DESSERTS

Mini Mud Cake

INGREDIENTS

4 tbsp plain flour
4 tbsp sugar
2 tbsp cocoa
1 egg
3 tbsp milk
3 tbsp oil

METHOD

1. Add dry ingredients to a large coffee mug and mix well.
2. Add the egg and mix thoroughly.
3. Pour in milk and oil and mix again.
4. Put your mug in the microwave and cook for 3 minutes on High.
5. The cake will rise over the top a little but don't worry.

You can add chocolate chips to it if you want double chocolate.

TIP

To make beating egg whites easier, add a pinch of salt.

DESSERTS

Moon Rocks

INGREDIENTS

250g milk chocolate
4 cups of Coco Pops or Rice Bubbles
200g white chocolate melts
2 cups mini marshmallows

METHOD

1. *Microwave the milk chocolate on High for 2 minutes, stirring every 30 seconds until almost fully melted.*
2. *Stir until chocolate is smooth and fully melted. Allow to cool slightly.*
3. *Mix together the Coco Pops/Rice Bubbles, white chocolate melts and marshmallows.*
4. *Add the melted chocolate. Be careful not to melt the marshmallows.*
5. *Put a little vegetable or olive oil on your fingers and roll the mixture into teaspoon-sized balls.*
6. *Place onto a tray lined with greaseproof paper or a paper patty cup.*
7. *Refrigerate until required.*

For something different, you could throw some raspberry jube lollies in the mix.

TIP

To get the most out of your lemons roll them firmly on a bench before juicing or cutting.

DESSERTS

Bread and Butter Hot Cross Buns

INGREDIENTS

6 hot cross buns
2 eggs
200ml milk
250g ready-made custard
2 tbsp sugar
Butter, to spread

METHOD

1. *Split the buns in half and butter both sides.*
2. *Place the bottom half of buns butter-side down into an oven-proof deep dish.*
3. *Combine the custard, eggs and milk.*
4. *Pour ½ the custard mix over the buns in the dish.*
5. *Put the top half of the buns on top.*
6. *Pour the remaining custard mixture over the tops of the buns.*
7. *Sprinkle the sugar over the top.*
8. *Bake in the oven at 160° for about 30 minutes or until the custard is set.*

This works especially good if the buns have become a bit stale.

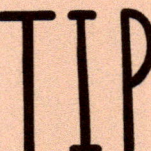

TIP

Try using a half-moon pizza cutter for cutting slices and brownies.

DESSERTS

Easy Vanilla Slice

INGREDIENTS

2 packets Malt'O'Milk biscuits
1 packet instant vanilla pudding mix
500ml thickened cream

METHOD

1. Line a slice tray with foil.
2. Line the tray with biscuit.
3. Mix the pudding with the cream and spread quickly over biscuits.
4. Put another layer of biscuit on top.
5. Put in the fridge until set.

You can ice the slice when set if desired.

www.ingramcontent.com/pod-product-compliance
Lightning Source LLC
Chambersburg PA
CBHW051323110526
44590CB00031B/4453